THE TIM VINE

BUMPER BOOK OF SILLINESS

This edition first published in Great Britain in 2013 by Orion Books
an imprint of the Orion Publishing Group Ltd
Orion House, 5 Upper St Martin's Lane,
London WC2H 9EA
An Hachette UK Company

10 9 8 7 6 5 4 3 2 1

A CIP catalogue record for this book is available from the British Library.

ISBN: 9781 4091 2760 4

Printed in China

Editorial: Jane Sturrock, Nicola Crossley and Helena Caldon
Art Direction: Helen Ewing
Design: Smith & Gilmour

Photographs © Startled Chameleon and Tim Vine, with the exception of page 10: Kobal Collection (top row, middle), Rex Features (top row, right).

Illustrations © Dan Fletcher: page 5, 8 (bottom), 15, 31 (black and white only), 42, (black and white only), 44, 48, 63, 66 (black and white only), 67, 75 (black and white only), 78 (top), 79 (middle), 85 (black and white only), 90 (black and white only), 109 (black and white only).

The Orion Publishing Group's policy is to use papers that are natural, renewable and recyclable and made from wood grown in sustainable forests. The logging and manufacturing processes are expected to conform to the environmental regulations of the country of origin.

www.orionbooks.co.uk

FOREWORD

HELLO VIEWERS!

IT'S TIM VINE HERE (IT'S YOU THERE). Welcome to my Bumper Book of Silliness. Put your 3D glasses on NOW. And then remove them because they won't make any difference. This is a bit like an annual. Annual love it. I've filled it with silly jokes, daft quizzes, zany pictures and silly daft zany other stuff too, as well, also. We live in a very serious world but now and again it's good to forget about that and say things like 'lozenge waffler' or 'giraffe sprocket'. Ideally to a stranger. See page 45 for other suggestions. Please ignore the following sentence which is written in capitals. ROUND WAY RIGHT THE IS WHICH PART ONLY THE IS THIS. I'm reminded of the words I said to my cousin, who half an hour previously had poured quick-drying cement on his own head. 'Don't be too hard on yourself. Go on, crack a smile.' As they used to say at my old school which didn't have a head boy – nobody's prefect. So, lovely readers, I hope this book tickles you. I have produced a limited edition on goose feathers to make that more achievable. Some people would rather read about magnets. I can't see the attraction.

Yours sillycerely,

Tim Vine

that's my signature tune

CONTENTS

FINGER ARCHERY

IT'S THE GAME EVERYONE IS TALKING ABOUT!
(… nearly everyone.) Archery with no need for a bow and
no need for dangerous sharp arrows. (The King said arise.
So he… arrows. I just thought of that. It doesn't matter.)
Yes, in this version of Robin Hood's favourite pastime, which
he also used to kill people, there is no risk of a trip to casualty.
The worst that can happen is a misplaced prod.

EQUIPMENT
**THE ARROW IS YOUR
INDEX FINGER**

**THE TARGET IS ON THE
OPPOSITE PAGE**

HOW TO PLAY

Place the target on a flat surface in front of you. Close your eyes
and start with your firing finger behind your back. On the instruction
'Fire', given by your opponent, bring your arm round swiftly and
keeping your eyes closed, bring your index finger down
towards the target.

SCORING

The first to score 37 points has won the game.
Traditionally in finger archery it is the first to 3
games who wins the set. And then it is the first to
14 sets who wins the match. If for some reason you
don't want to play 14 sets, you can decide the contest
by who is wearing the highest socks. Closest to the
knee wins. But if your socks go beyond the knee they
are void. In which case, you are not allowed to fold your
socks back over themselves to make them shorter.

THE TARGET

SAFETY

When you are playing a game DO NOT point your finger at your opponent. Because it is rude.

10

2

6

TIM'S TIPS

Do not be disappointed if it takes you a while to get the hang of it.

TIM VINE'S AUTOGRAPH

| | I DON'T REALLY LIKE IT | I QUITE LIKE IT | I LIKE IT | I LIKE IT A LOT | I LOVE IT LIKE IT |

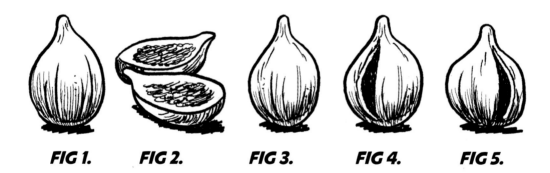

FIG 1.   FIG 2.   FIG 3.   FIG 4.   FIG 5.

THESE ARE PICTURES OF FIGS

WHERE'S WALLABY?

Here is a page of kangaroos. Except one of them is a wallaby.
But which one?

Answer: I'm not sure because they look really similar, don't they?

HOW TO CATCH A PEN BEHIND YOUR EAR

The aim is to send the pen through one complete rotation in the air and then have it land behind your ear.

The first and most important element of the manoeuvre is the landing area – The Ear. The bigger and more protruding the ear the larger the landing area. And too much hair around the ear area is also a disadvantage.

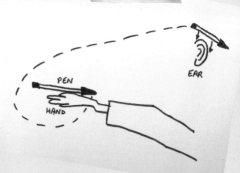

EXAMPLES OF GOOD EARS:

EXAMPLES OF BAD EARS:

Smaller ears perhaps look nicer socially but for 'pen behind the ear', they are not good.

THE THROW

Hold the pen flat across the fingers of your open hand with the lid towards you. The lid is the extra bit of weight that drives the pen round in a somersault and hopefully onto the ear. When you are ready, jerk your forearm upwards and launch the pen towards your ear, tilting the pen bottom first as it leaves your palm. If it has landed correctly you should now have a pen behind your ear with the lid facing back towards your shoulder.

Don't worry if you don't get it the first few times. Even the experts can sometimes take 4 or 5 minutes before a successful docking.

You may find the whole process made easier with repetitive music on in the background. 'Pen behind the ear, pen behind the ear, pen behind the ear, pen behind the ear.'

POPCORN BOXING

THE LATEST IN FOOD SPORT COMBINING SPEED, FITNESS AND A POPULAR SNACK.

WHAT YOU'LL NEED

POPCORN SEEDS

VEGETABLE OIL

BOXING GLOVES

INSTRUCTIONS

Put the popcorn seeds at the bottom of a saucepan in a small amount of vegetable oil. Turn on the heat. At this point you would normally cover the pan with a lid. **DON'T DO THIS.** As the popcorn begins to pop up out of the saucepan, start swinging.

Over time your reactions will start to improve and you will get more and more direct hits. Then you can branch out into other popcorn sports.

POPCORN BASEBALL

POPCORN SQUASH

POPCORN DARTS

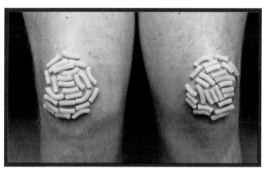

THE HISTORY OF LEGS

Nobody is sure of the exact date that legs were invented although they are thought to be predate arms which means they were almost certainly first used before 1974.

A LEG OF DARTS

MACARONI KNEES

Early use of legs is thought to mainly involve walking and running. This is the same today where the traditional alternation of left leg and right leg would have the effect of transporting the torso and head forwards and/or backwards.

It is not clear if any other method was preferred in the past and certainly if little jumps with the feet together was ever used – it has never been as effective as left, right, left, right and was therefore phased out over time. Garden birds, however, still use the feet-together hopping system which seems to suit them because they have springy kneecaps.

THIS IS A GENUINE PHOTO OF TIM'S LEGS. LOOK AT THE WIDTH BETWEEN THEM.

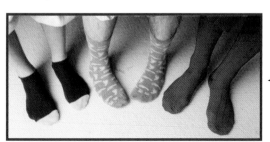

EXTRA FOOTAGE

THE ADVENTURES OF PUNSLINGER

COWBOY OH COWBOY
IS HE PUNNY!

IT WAS A BLISTERING DAY...

OOH ME BLISTERS ARE KILLING ME.

THE SUN WAS BEATING DOWN...

I'VE GOT FOUR ACES, MR DOWN.

THE HEAT WAS EVEN AFFECTING THE COWBOY LAUNDERETTE.

THE TUMBLEWEED DRIER IS BROKEN.

AND THEN...

WHY AM I VISUALLY FLICKERING ON AND OFF?

THE SHERIFF STROBED INTO TOWN...

FOLLOWED BY AN UNUSUAL SOUND APPROACHING...

CLIP CLIP

CLIP CLIP

IT SOUNDS LIKE A TWO-LEGGED HORSE.

OR A FOUR-LEGGED HORSE GOING ROUND A CORNER TOO FAST.

IT'S ME, PUNSLINGER!

THE WHOLE TOWN CHEERS.

!HOORAY!

I'M CUTTING MY NAILS AND MY HORSE IS WEARING SLIPPERS.

CLIP CLIP

SILENT FEET

I'M GETTING READY FOR A DATE AND I DON'T MEAN I'M PREPARING TO EAT A DRIED PRUNE.

ANOTHER PUN...

NOT A PLUM, A PRUNE.

WHAT SHALL I GIVE MY GIRL IRIS AS A PRESENT?

A FLOWER?

NO, SHE'S A HUMAN.

SHERIFF, YOU KEEP MOVING FROM ONE SAND HILL TO ANOTHER. YOU'VE CHANGED YOUR DUNE!

I COULD DO WITH A SHANDY.

WHERE YOU'RE SHTANDING LOOKS VERY SHANDY ALREADY.

I WAS TRYING TO SAY, GET IRIS A FLOWER LIKE A ROSE.

GREAT IDEA! PUT YOUR FOOT ON THE PETAL. LET'S GO TO THE FLOWER SHOP!

NO PUNSLINGER, WE DON'T SELL MARRIED RED ROSES AS WELL. THAT'S NOT WHAT I MEANT BY A SINGLE RED ROSE.

SHE'LL LOVE THIS ANYWAY. LET'S GO!

PUNSLINGER ROSE OFF WITH A RODE IN HIS HAND.

OTHER WAY ROUND.

BUT AS HE WENT, THE SUN GOT HOTTER.

I'M SWEATING BUCKETS.

CLANK

AND HOTTER...

THIS IS LIKE DEAF VALLEY.

PARDON?

AND EVEN HOTTER.

MY HEART'S MELTING.

THIS IS NO TIME FOR ROMANCE.

HANG ON! OH NO, LOOK.

THE ROSE HAS WILTED.

STAND UP WILT THOU . . .

THE BEAUTIFUL PIGMENT IS SAGGING.

IT'S THE DROOPING OF THE COLOUR.

IRIS WILL THINK I DON'T LOVE HER AND WHERE'S THE PUN IN THAT?

PUNSLINGER AND HIS HORSE SAT NEXT TO A LARGE CLIFF.

SHE'S JUST A DEVIL WOMAN. ♫ ♫

MODERN REFERENCE

✗

BUT . . .

HEY LOOK! A CLOUD! IF IT STARTS RAINING THAT WOULD BE CHAMPION.

NB: RAINING REIGNING.

THE BUMPER BOOK OF SILLINESS

BUT...

SWIRLING WIND

SWIRLING WIND

SWOOSH

WE'VE MISSED THE CUMULO NIM **BUS**.

TURN ROUND!

SWIISH

WHAT A POUR SHOW.

SWOOSH

STOP CLOUDING ABOUT!

THE CLOUD DIDN'T HAVE A SILVER VINING AND SOON LEFT.

HEY LOOK, THERE'S A WATERING CAN!

NO IT'S NOT. IT'S A MIRAGE. IF IT WAS A REAL WATERING CAN THAT WOMAN WOULD PICK IT UP AND POUR ALL THE WATER THAT'S IN IT ONTO HER FLOWERS.

OH!

NO WATERING CAN DO.

NOW EMPTY

DIZZY UP! I MEAN GIDDY UP. THERE'S ONE LAST PLACE WE CAN GO.

LATER...

THE BUCKET DOESN'T REACH THE WATER.

IT'S BEYOND THE PALE.

THAT'S IT THEN. IT'S THE END OF THE ROSE. IRIS WILL LEAVE ME WHEN SHE SEES THIS. WITHER I LIKE IT OR NOT.

SNIFF WEEP BLUBBER

BUT AS THE TEARS FELL, SOME OF THEM LANDED ON THE ROSE AND...

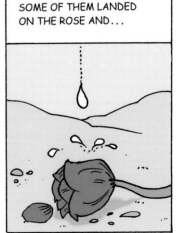

BIT...

BY BIT...

THE ROSE ROSE.

IT STEMMED FROM HERE

YES IT'S ENDED IN TEARS AND AS A RESULT IT HASN'T.

IRIS ARRIVES.

HI PUNSLINGER, WHAT A LOVELY FLOWER.

I'VE SPRINKLED ITALIAN INSECTS ON IT TOO. I KNOW YOU LIKE ROME ANTS.

YOU'VE MADE ME VERY HAPPY. HAVE SOME EDAM.

CHEESY GRIN

!HOORAY!

THERE'S ALWAYS ONE...

THE END

HOW COME I DIDN'T APPEAR ON THIS LAST PAGE? I WAS AN INTEGRAL PART OF THE STORY.

GLADIATOR

SADIATOR

HOW PLANET EARTH HAS CHANGED IN THE LAST 100 YEARS

1912	1913	1914	1915	1916	1917
1918	1919	1920	1921	1922	1923
1924	1925	1926	1927	1928	1929
1930	1931	1932	1933	1934	1935
1936	1937	1938	1939	1940	1941
1942	1943	1944	1945	1946	1947
1948	1949	1950	1951	1952	1953
1954	1955	1956	1957	1958	1959

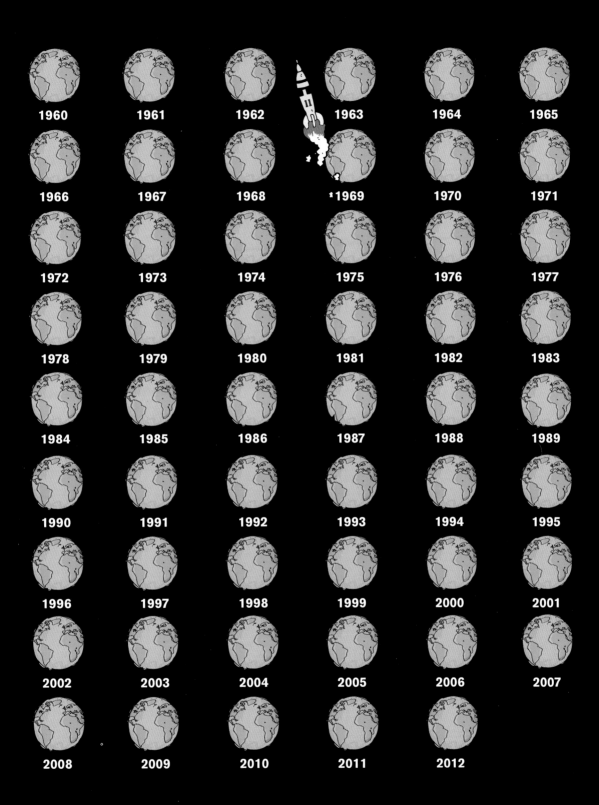

1960   1961   1962   1963   1964   1965

1966   1967   1968   *1969   1970   1971

1972   1973   1974   1975   1976   1977

1978   1979   1980   1981   1982   1983

1984   1985   1986   1987   1988   1989

1990   1991   1992   1993   1994   1995

1996   1997   1998   1999   2000   2001

2002   2003   2004   2005   2006   2007

2008   2009   2010   2011   2012

CARTOONS

LEEDS

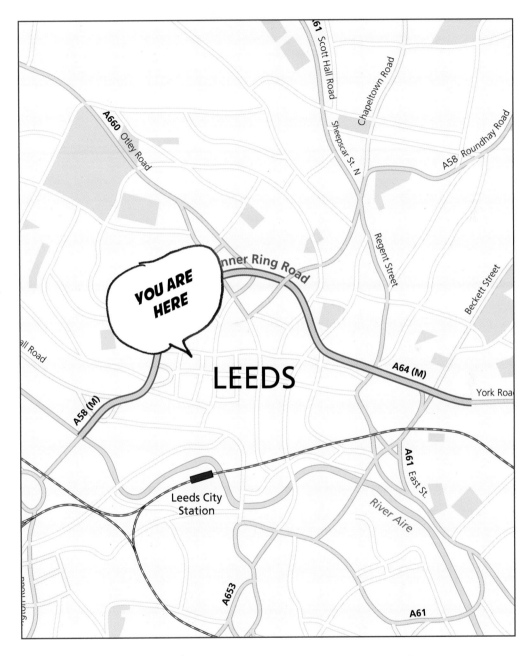

**THIS ONLY APPLIES TO PEOPLE FROM LEEDS.
IF YOU ARE FROM BIRMINGHAM PLEASE TURN OVER.**

LEEDS

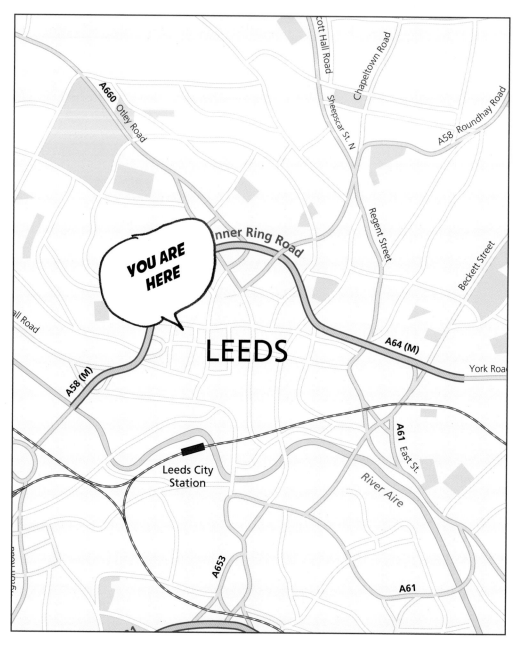

**THIS ONLY APPLIES TO PEOPLE FROM BIRMINGHAM
WHO ARE VISITING LEEDS.**

I saw this large fish playing guitar in a subway.
It was a busking shark.

Where's the best place to lean a sea-lion ladder?
Up against a walrus.

I saw a postman on the beach. He was making a sand parcel.

This dinghy said to a wave, do you want to go out with me?
And the wave said, I'm afraid I can't because I'm tide up.

I saw King Canute on the beach with his laptop.
He was hitting Control C.

What's a crustacean's favourite football team? Shellsea.

You know when there's two flags stuck in the beach and there's
a sign that says ONLY SWIM BETWEEN THESE FLAGS?
I don't know about you but I always ignore it and swim in the sea.

It's hard to tell when a lobster is sunburnt because
he already looks like a lobster.

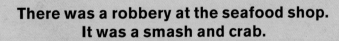

There was a robbery at the seafood shop.
It was a smash and crab.

I saw a quiche floating in the water.
I thought, that's flan buoyant.

TIM WEARING A MOTOR BOATER

THEY MAY BE WARM AND CUDDLY BUT BEWARE. IT'S IMPOSSIBLE TO PREDICT....

P.T.O. ⇨

WHEN SOFT TOYS ATTACK

FURNITURE FOOTWEAR

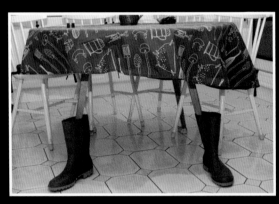

A kitchen table in wellingtons

A foot cushion in Hush Puppies

A conservatory chair in trainers

An antique writing desk in DM's

A television cabinet in slippers

CARTOONS

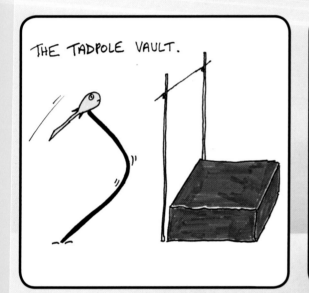

THE TADPOLE VAULT.

CARTONS

JOKES ABOUT... TECHNOLOGY

What do you call a Welsh singer who never gets lost?
Tom Tom Jones.

I think my computer has been hacked into.
There's an axe sticking out of it.

I order toast online. It's quite easy, although you get
a lot of pop ups.

Apparently playing too many computer games can
make you paranoid. Is there someone on the roof?

I'm not a big fan of social networking. I think it's
important to sit down face to face with your androids.

So I said to my bank manager, you promised me fun
banking and I'm not feeling it. He said no, what I said
was phone banking.

My sat nav got stuck down the toilet. Now I've got
nowhere to go.

Last time I put my credit card in a machine, it said
authorising and J.K. Rowling took off in a hot air
balloon.

I'm very pleased with my new milking machine.
It works a teat.

SING-A-LONG WITH TIM

DEEP

[A SONG ABOUT HOW DEEP THE OCEAN IS]

CHORUS

> *D7*
> Deep very deep very deep very deep
> *G*
> the ocean is deep
> *D7*
> much deeper than you think

X2

D7
Ask a mackerel and he say DEEP *G7*
D7
ask a dolphin and he say DEEP *G7*
D7
ask a great white and he say DEEP *G7*
A7
ask all the prawns and they'll all repeat it's…

CHORUS

D7
Ask a walrus and he say DEEP *G7*
D7
ask a starfish and he say DEEP *G7*
D7
ask a blue whale and he say DEEP *G7*
A7
ask all the shrimps and they'll repeat it's…

CHORUS

ENDS on *D7* and a sheepish smile

PAIRS OF WORDS

[TO SAY TO A STRANGER]

1. Mars cardigan
2. Trumpet cringe
3. Flannel spanner
4. Coconut chimney
5. Stern buttercup
6. Banana sellotape
7. Piglet highlighter
8. Zinc pixie
9. Ankle crumb-flyer
10. Skip gristle
11. Aniseed cropswitch
12. Snooze clacker
13. Satchel giblets
14. Flob dongle
15. Ben Nevis
16. Parsnip calendar
17. Schnitzel baggage
18. Chiplock mandarin
19. Lug tap
20. Inca doughnut
21. Tangerine squirrel
22. Rotation pants
23. Crank mango
24. Gesture wok
25. Weetabix vicar
26. Whisky waders
27. Rather hog
28. Bangle soup

Extra pairs:

Landslide pickler

Umpire forceps

Loft bloomer

UPCOMING EVENTS

A COCONUT CONKERS TOURNAMENT
24TH OCTOBER

A MEETING OF THE FATHERS FOR JUST ICE

LIVE IN CONCERT
Russian Punk Singer

VLADMIR PUKIN

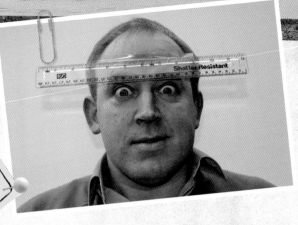

THE HEIGHT OF SUMMER ➤ I SUMMER

MOON WIND FARM.

THE WIDTH OF WINTER ➤ WINTER

THE CIRCUMFERENCE OF AUTUMN ➤ AUTUMN

LAURA ASHLEY'S SPRING COLLECTION

LAURA LIVES IN SUTTON

stars and space

The first animal they sent into space was a monkey.
They asked him if he wanted anything to eat and he
went bananas.

I came second in an astronomy competition.
I got a constellation prize.

Did you know if you misbehave when you're flying
a rocket, you have to sit on the astronaughty step.

Apparently in space there is zero gravity, which means
up there you can't take anything seriously.

Did you know if you should find a bath big enough
to put Saturn in, the planet would float. Mind you, when
you take it out it would leave terrible rings.

Sometimes the sun gets stuck in my toilet.
Ah, the wonders of the solar cistern.

Mercury is a planet and also the name of a metal.
I wonder if there's a planet somewhere called
stainless steel?

If you fly a rocket, don't forget to shuttle the doors.

So I said to this astronaut, what do they say
to you just before you launch? He said blast off.
I said I was only asking.

TIM VINE

CROSSWORD SEARCH

Hidden in this grid are some words and phrases people say when they're cross. Can you find all 15?

B	T	O	K	V	E	X	Z	E	O	S	H	O	V	E	I	T
Y	Q	S	R	L	R	E	N	R	A	N	Y	L	L	I	S	N
G	F	L	I	P	P	I	N	G	F	L	A	M	E	R	S	O
L	O	K	W	A	F	H	S	I	Q	I	X	B	Y	U	E	J
Z	T	Y	P	I	C	A	L	P	D	B	K	A	M	L	V	C
O	W	B	A	L	D	E	R	D	A	S	H	C	D	P	O	Q
P	L	E	R	M	I	T	B	E	X	I	O	W	P	I	B	N
K	G	A	E	Y	K	P	Q	U	E	D	V	O	O	W	A	R
N	R	Y	H	A	W	H	A	T	I	R	M	P	E	I	S	A
O	R	U	T	B	I	C	W	M	O	A	P	W	L	S	N	D
U	R	T	O	R	X	H	O	J	P	T	E	B	K	J	E	K
W	R	U	B	C	I	E	K	W	C	B	Q	X	C	P	V	I
S	F	G	H	U	T	M	Y	F	O	O	T	C	I	M	A	R
H	U	K	O	Z	M	E	Y	Q	P	Z	F	N	P	E	E	P
N	W	O	N	K	E	V	A	H	T	H	G	I	M	I	H	Q
L	N	O	N	S	E	N	S	E	M	A	R	J	O	R	I	E

1 Typical

2 Drat

3 Oh bother

4 What

5 Flipping flamers

6 Darn

7 Heavens above

8 Nonsense Marjorie

9 Shove it

10 Grrrr

11 My foot

12 Silly narner

13 Balderdash

14 Pickle

15 I might have known

Different ways of waiting at a bus stop

Spot the Similarity

**There are over 3000 similarities
between these two pictures.
How many can you find?**

WHAT DO AMERICAN FOOTBALLERS DO ON THEIR DAY OFF?

It's a tough question, isn't it? A bit like 'why does a fireman point a hose at the flames?' Nobody is really sure. So we followed Irvin for a day. Irvin is an American footballer who plays for the Ohio Wombats.

AMERICAN FOOTBALL SUPER LEAGUE

In the morning Irvin placed his hands on a piano and didn't move them.

Then Irvin got stuck in a child's slide.

For lunch Irvin had a barbeque. (Note the lack of food and heat.)

Irvin spent the afternoon pushing an empty wheelbarrow round the garden.

halfords
Rapid Digital Tyre Inflator

Then Irvin adjusted his watch next to the tool shed where he keeps his rapid digital tyre inflator.

As the sun went down on an eventful day, Irvin waited for his mum to get back from work.

If you are interested, Irvin has his own fan page. It's on a sheet of A4 and he keeps it in a biscuit tin under his bed. He's got three names on it. Two if you don't count his mother. None if you don't count himself and his mother's friend, Leonard.

MOUSTACHE DRYING

TIM VINE

CAUGHT JESTER

HILARY CLINTON PAINTING HEAVY WEAPONRY

That's nice art Hilary.*

* The joke is that 'art Hilary' sounds a bit like artillery.

FOOD MOMENTS

ISN'T IT ANNOYING WHEN YOU'VE LOST THE LABEL OFF A JAR AND YOU CAN'T REMEMBER WHAT'S IN IT?

SOMETIMES, AT THE END OF A MEAL IN A RESTAURANT, INSTEAD OF GIVING THE WAITRESS A TIP I GIVE HER A *FELT*-TIP. IT'S ALWAYS REALLY FUNNY.

THE SECOND PICTURE CAPTURES THE MOMENT THAT I WAS TOLD WHAT I THOUGHT WAS A CARROT JUICE WAS IN FACT A GOLDFISH SMOOTHIE.

COLOURING IN

WHY NOT HAVE A GO AT COLOURING THIS IN:

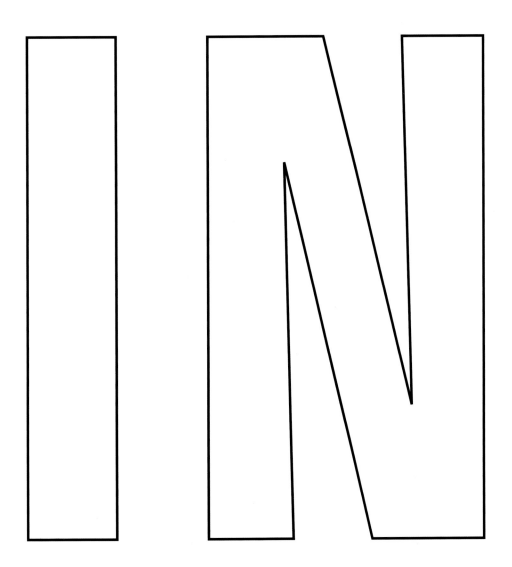

EXAMPLES OF COLOURING IN:

EDIBLE OR POISONOUS?
THOSE ALL-IMPORTANT RESULTS

STRAWBERRY

EDIBLE

TOAST

EDIBLE

POISON

POISONOUS

WOTSIT

EDIBLE

MUSHROOM

DEPENDS

CRUMB

EDIBLE

LEMON

EDIBLE

BIRTHDAY CAKE

EDIBLE

SNOW WHITE'S APPLE, KINDLY GIVEN TO HER BY OLD WOMAN

EDIBLE

EVERY ATTEMPT HAS BEEN MADE BY THE AUTHOR TO VERIFY THESE RESULTS. HOWEVER, SHOULD THERE BE ANY MISTAKES ON THIS CHART THE PUBLISHER CANNOT BE HELD RESPONSIBLE

CAPTAIN OVER - REACTION

CAPTAIN, JUST SO YOU KNOW, I BORROWED YOUR NEWSPAPER EARLIER.

WHAT!

I PUT IT BACK

AAAAH

I ONLY READ ONE ARTICLE

NO PLEASE NO...

I THOUGHT YOU WOULDN'T MIND.

MMM... SNIFF... YOU...OH MOTHER OF MERCY...

...AAAAH

IT'S ONLY A NEWSPAPER.

GET AN AMBULANCE.

CAR PARKARAOKE

DOT TO DOT
FOR BEGINNERS

JOIN THE DOTS TO DRAW A WASHING LINE:

•   •

JOIN THE DOTS TO DRAW THE LONDON TO GLASGOW TRAIN LINE:

•

•

JOIN THE DOTS TO DRAW SOME RYVITA:

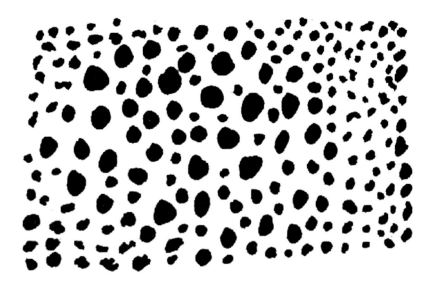

My vehicle's got acne. It's a tran zit van.

I've got a sports car. He's really good at tennis, netball and cricket.

I missed my train this morning so in the evening I went back to the station to spend some more time with it.

I saw a car made of knives. It was good at sharp turns.

How do you say goodbye to a lorry? So long vehicle.

I bought an electric car. I've crashed into my kettle three times.

You can't take speedway drivers seriously. They're always skidding around.

What do rabbits go on holiday in? A carrot van.

I know a bloke who deliberately runs people over in German cars. He's a mer-sadist.

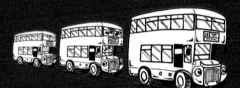

TIM VINE

LOW COST HOLIDAY

LOCUST HOLIDAY

COLOURING INN

WHY NOT HAVE A GO AT COLOURING THIS INN:

EXAMPLES OF COLOURING INN:

SING-A-LONG WITH TIM
THE LADDER SONG

(YOU CAN ACTUALLY CLIMB UP AND DOWN A LADDER DURING THE CHORUSES. ALTHOUGH YOU SHOULD NOT ATTEMPT THIS WHILE PLAYING A PIANO.)

Everybody has wishes, everybody has hopes,
Some are small like dishes, some are big like boats,
All I ever wanted since the day I was born
Is to have my own ladder.
Then one day in the post, a box arrived at the door
And inside was this ladder all I dreamt of and more,
So without hesitation I said cheerio floor
And then everyone saw me.

Go up my ladder, one step I've done it,
Go up my ladder, two steps I've done it,
Go up my ladder, three steps I've done it,
Now I'm on the summit.

As I stood at the top I saw the beautiful view,
And my friends were all waving so I waved at them too
But the weirdest thing happened when I saw them all smile,
I began to get lonely.
You see the top of my ladder wasn't nice anymore,
I was up there alone, my friends were all on the floor.
They were having a party and I couldn't join in,
So I made my decision.

Go down my ladder, one step I've done it,
Go down my ladder, two steps I've done it,
Go down my ladder, three steps I've done it,
Now I'm back where I began it.
My ladder!

Ends with a sheepish smile

his? NO! That.

OLYMPIC RINGS?
NO.
FROG SPAWN.

AN ARCHWAY MADE OF
BARBED WIRE?
NO.
TINSEL IN THE WIND.

A RECTANGLE?
NO.
A SQUARE, SIDE ON.

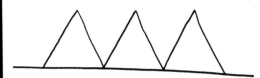

THREE PYRAMIDS?
NO.
THE LETTER 'W' HELD IN
PLACE BY TWO GUY ROPES.

THE BACK OF SOMEONE'S
HEAD?
NO.
A LONG FRINGE.

A TRUCK WITHOUT WHEELS?
NO.
A BED WITH A SCHOOL DESK
ON IT.

EAR MUFFS BENT OUT OF
SHAPE?
NO.
A ROAD CONNECTING TWO
MASSIVE BLACK BLOBS.

IF MONTHS WERE PEOPLE

JANUARY

FEBRUARY

MARCH

APRIL

MAY

JUNE

JULY

AUGUST

SEPTEMBER

OCTOBER

NOVEMBER

DECEMBER

JOKES ABOUT...
SCHOOL

One of my subjects at school was watering plants. My report said 'could do wetter'.

I came from a very strict school. In the school play you had to put your hand up before you said your line.

We didn't do history at my school. The headmaster said it was a thing of the past.

In the final lesson of term, as a treat, our ghost story teacher used to read us some maths.

Pupils nowadays don't use sheets of paper, they use a computer. My dad tried it once but when he made a mistake he screwed up the laptop and threw it in the bin.

In one lesson I had to tell the other pupils they'd been permanently suspended. It was an expelling test.

My maths teacher also taught us swimming. We used to dive in off a ruler.

When I got my timetable one of the lessons was called DIV. I thought it was divinity but it turned out they just thought I was thick.

I remember one lesson when the teacher used to push my shoulder whenever I was trying to write something. It was joggraphy.

I once cycled to school every day for a week. I don't know why. It was half term.

Biscuits wearing hats

And what a way to start the ball rolling with these four! First up it's sponge finger wearing a stylish red woollen bobble hat. Next to him, making a splash in yellow, there's Highland shortbread donning the latest in swimming caps. Garibaldi, meanwhile, opts for a lime green, traditional Chinese hat (he would, wouldn't he!) while party ring leans on the wall beside him in a high end ascot dress hat finished off with a plastic diamond. Wonderful!

Looks like someone's booked a table at The Ritz! It's fig roll à la Fred Astaire in a tilted top hat. That's effortless.

What's that noise? Could it be your heart racing for biscuits in uniform? Here's Jammie Dodger enforcing the law and next to him in an airline pilot hat, the commanding presence and slimline figure of chocolate finger.

Ginger nut we salute you. That summer hat is pure biscuit style. Nobody does it better. And who's this windswept Audrey Hepburn? Utterly nonchalant, not a crumb in sight. Devastating bourbon.

And finally, only rich tea could carry off this look. A nun's habit. It just seems to work but you don't know why.

LET'S HEAR IT ONE MORE TIME FOR BISCUITS WEARING HATS!

ADVERTS

FUNFAIR FOR GOATS!
They deserve to have fun too.
Includes Big Wheel, Dodgems and Goats Train.

Your goat will need to be accompanied at all times by an adult. An adult human not an adult goat. **STRICTLY NO SHEEP.**

SMOKE ALARM ALARM.

Tells you when your smoke alarm has gone off.
(Also reacts to whispering).

CAMP AMNESIA!
For the holiday you'll never remember.
Now where was I . . .?

TIM VINE

CUTLERY FOR THE BIG EATER

IT'S MASSIVE CUTLERY BASICALLY.

DINGHY SHOES

Walk on water without the aid of a miracle. Do not wear while jumping up and down on a bed of nails.

METAL SOCKS

Next time you stub your toe you'll laugh.

PERUVIAN HATS

They're peruvian to be very popular!

They cover the top of your head!

People from Peru Swear in them!

ALTERNATIVE USES FOR...
A GRAPEFRUIT

Cufflinks

A lid for your mustard

A pillow

The yellow ball in a game of snooker

A small planet for a moose

You can even use it to improve your local area. Where a yellow line has got worn away a grapefruit fills the gap perfectly

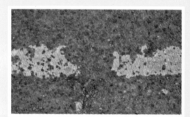

Before

After

'THAT'S MUSIC TO MY EARS'

Someone playing violin

It's a well-known phrase but strangely it's rarely said when somebody is listening to music. Surely when the soundwaves of music reach a person's ear drums and it is correctly identified by their brain, this would be the ideal moment to say 'that's music to my ears?'

Someone playing piano

I bought a christian keyboard the other day. It's called a Thesizer. It was called a Synthesizer but the sin has been removed.

Someone playing piano with a violin

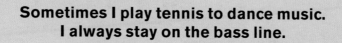

JOKES ABOUT... SPORT

I entered the 'interfering in other people's business' Olympics.
I got a meddle.

Sometimes I play tennis to dance music.
I always stay on the bass line.

Have you heard of that game where you
take your eye out and put it in a sock. It's called eye socky.

My dad worked in a bank and he also did gymnastics.
He used to practise with the vault.

So I was playing football with a priest and I was
booked for a late tabernacle.

People say I'm too agressive when I play games just because the last
time I played I broke my arm. Admittedly it was a game of darts.

I watched a witch playing different sports. It was wicked.

I've invented a new version of football where instead of kicking
the ball you hit it with a basket. I call it basketball.

It's important to warm up before playing sport.
Unless you're playing a game of 'Igloo roof crawling'.

Wayne Rooney used to practise his football skills by kicking a ball
against a brick wall. I did the same thing with the javelin.

EASY STUNTS

DO TRY THIS AT HOME

HOOVERING WITH ONE EYE CLOSED

OPEN A DOOR JUST USING YOUR FOOT

HOLDING YOUR HAND IN THE FRIDGE FOR ONE MINUTE

REALLY, REALLY, REALLY GENTLY TAP ONE OF YOUR TEETH WITH A ROLLING PIN

BALANCE A TEA BAG ON YOUR NOSE

TIM VINE

CLAP WITH SOCKS ON YOUR HANDS

TOUCH YOUR FINGER ON AN EXPENSIVE ORNAMENT

TURN THE RADIO DOWN REALLY LOW AND TRY TO HEAR WHAT THEY ARE SAYING

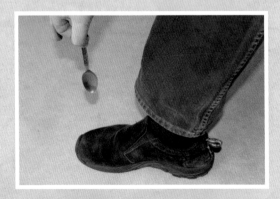

DROP A TEASPOON ON YOUR FOOT. (MAKE SURE YOU'RE WEARING SHOES OTHERWISE IT MIGHT HURT)

SHUT A BOOK ON YOUR THUMB

EDWARD POST-IT NOTE HANDS

TIM VINE

Edward was out walking one morning …

when suddenly something startled him.

It was a small shrub.

He didn't like it but he couldn't think why.

Then it dawned on him.

So he dashed back inside,

and returned with a pad of Post-it notes.

He decorated the shrub.

That's better, thought Edward. Much better.

JOKES ABOUT...
FURNITURE

I keep my ornaments on an imaginary shelf above my fireplace. It's the mental piece.

Two armchairs had a race. It was a photo furnish.

When I was a kid, whenever I jumped up and down on my bed I nearly broke my neck. I was on the bottom bunk.

I bought a cabinet. I caught seven cabbies.

So I said to this bloke, can you fix my kitchen unit? He said, 'What did you call me?'

I went to a 1970s furniture shop. They had everything by the kitsch sink.

All my chairs and tables are made of bracken. It's my fernature.

I saw an Italian actress covered in cushions. It was Sofa Loren.

I went to a shop that restores furniture to its original condition. I gave them my pine wardrobe and two days later they gave me a fir tree.

I used to live in a removals van. Not much space, no windows, but some lovely furniture.

WHICH OF THESE Would You MOST LIKE TO SWIM IN?

A

B

C

d

E

F

IT'S MULTI-POOL CHOICE

SO YOU WANT TO BE A RADIATOR...

1 In order to be a radiator you need to have a wall and you need to be a source of heat. So your first job is to find the wall that you are happy to be a radiator on.

2 Once you have chosen your location you must become hot. There's no point being a cold radiator. It's about as much use as an uphill slide or an underwater fireplace. As we know, the best source of heat is a hot water bottle.

3 Obviously it would be ridiculous to use one of these to heat a room. You will need at least five of them.

4 Fill each hot water bottle with hot water.

5 Using gaffer tape, fix the hot water bottles to your body.

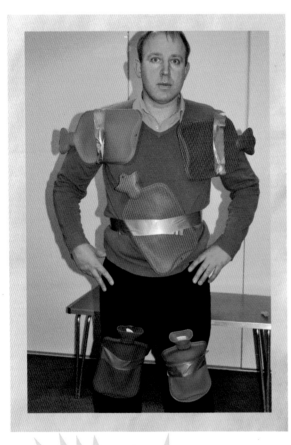

6 Now you will need to start working quite quickly because over a reasonably short period of time the hot water bottles will go cold. Position yourself in front of your wall.

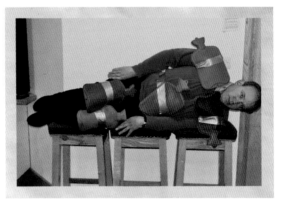

7 If you want you can add a cosmetic front to give it the finishing touch. That's it. You're heating the room and people will love it. It reminds me of the time someone hid my radiator and challenged me to find it. When I got close to it they said 'You're getting warmer.'

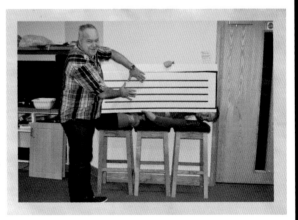

WELL DONE!
YOU'RE A
RADIATOR.

Bedtime Story

The Story Of A Bed

Once upon a time there was a bed. He was a double bed called Edward. It would have made sense to shorten his name to Ed. Then he would have been Ed the bed, but Edward hated having his name shortened. He was Edward the bed. Never Ed. 'I'm Edward,' he would say. 'If I was in a story I would be Ed, but I'm not,' Edward, like all fictional characters, didn't know he was in a story.

Edward was married to a single bed called Myrtle. They had just given birth to bunk beds. The top bunk was called Toppy and the bottom bunk was called Michael because Bottomy didn't sound right. They were the beds belonging to Mr Craven and his family who, to avoid confusion, were humans.

On the morning in question (what question?), the Craven family had gone on holiday, so Edward and Myrtle had the horse to themselves. Sorry, had the house to themselves. That was a typing error. Edward decided it was time his family took a holiday too and he was going to organise it, seeing as he was the bed winner. 'What we need is a vacation, a chance to relax and take the weight off our sheet,' announced Edward. 'But where can we go Daddy?' said Toppy. 'Every hotel is fully booked. They've already got beds'. 'Don't worry', said Edward, 'we'll think of something, I'm sure'. 'Let's hope so', said Michael, 'This story goes on for another three pages.'

Just then there was a knock on the door. It was their old friend Gooseberry the Octopus. They had met him four years ago at an aquarium where Gooseberry worked on the till in the gift shop. 'Hello Gooseberry,' said Edward, inviting him in

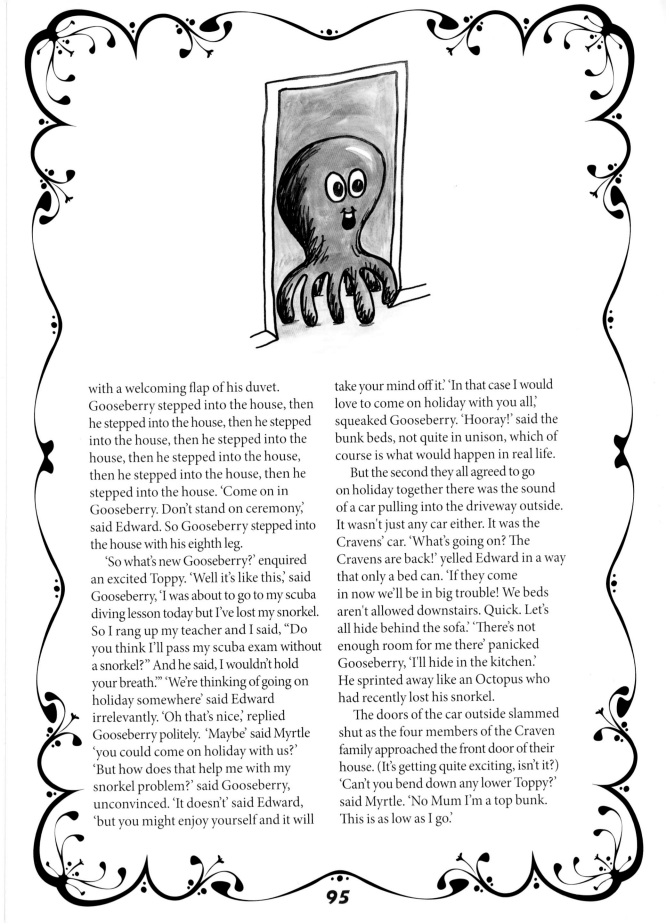

with a welcoming flap of his duvet. Gooseberry stepped into the house, then he stepped into the house, then he stepped into the house, then he stepped into the house, then he stepped into the house, then he stepped into the house, then he stepped into the house. 'Come on in Gooseberry. Don't stand on ceremony,' said Edward. So Gooseberry stepped into the house with his eighth leg.

'So what's new Gooseberry?' enquired an excited Toppy. 'Well it's like this,' said Gooseberry, 'I was about to go to my scuba diving lesson today but I've lost my snorkel. So I rang up my teacher and I said, "Do you think I'll pass my scuba exam without a snorkel?" And he said, I wouldn't hold your breath."' 'We're thinking of going on holiday somewhere' said Edward irrelevantly. 'Oh that's nice,' replied Gooseberry politely. 'Maybe' said Myrtle 'you could come on holiday with us?' 'But how does that help me with my snorkel problem?' said Gooseberry, unconvinced. 'It doesn't' said Edward, 'but you might enjoy yourself and it will

take your mind off it.' 'In that case I would love to come on holiday with you all,' squeaked Gooseberry. 'Hooray!' said the bunk beds, not quite in unison, which of course is what would happen in real life.

But the second they all agreed to go on holiday together there was the sound of a car pulling into the driveway outside. It wasn't just any car either. It was the Cravens' car. 'What's going on? The Cravens are back!' yelled Edward in a way that only a bed can. 'If they come in now we'll be in big trouble! We beds aren't allowed downstairs. Quick. Let's all hide behind the sofa.' 'There's not enough room for me there' panicked Gooseberry, 'I'll hide in the kitchen.' He sprinted away like an Octopus who had recently lost his snorkel.

The doors of the car outside slammed shut as the four members of the Craven family approached the front door of their house. (It's getting quite exciting, isn't it?) 'Can't you bend down any lower Toppy?' said Myrtle. 'No Mum I'm a top bunk. This is as low as I go.'

10 things to do to make you happy

1. Hum in a field.

2. Lean out of a bus and shout 'This is the life!'

3. Smell coffee granules then smell a lemon. Alternate.

4. Start laughing for no reason and keep laughing until it feels natural.

5. Buy yourself a present. Wrap it up and then don't open it until you've forgotten what it is.

6. Eat a tiramisu, with your feet in a bucket of hot water.

7. Say nice things to a horse.

8. Lie on your back on some grass and sing 'We've only just begun'.

9. Walk into a nightclub, dance like crazy to one song and then leave.

10. Go into your garden at dawn and join in whistling with the birds.

TIM VINE

100

FROM THE PEOPLE WHO BROUGHT YOU 'BEFORE THEY WERE FAMOUS', IT'S...

BEFORE THEY WERE FARMERS

BEFORE LEN GROB WAS A FARMER HE WAS THE FILM STAR GREGORY PECK.

BEFORE RICK GERRARD WAS A FARMER HE WAS THE AMERICAN COMEDIENNE LUCILLE BALL.

BEFORE MARK SANDERS WAS A FARMER HE WAS LEN GROB'S GARDENER.

ADVERTS

THE CARTWHEEL TRAINER!

The wooden frame that improves your cartwheels.

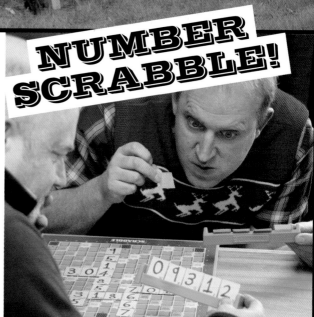

ALTERNATIVE USES FOR...

A TOOTHBRUSH

A MAP POINTER.

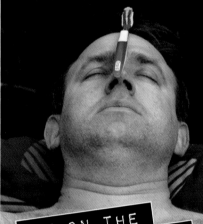

PUT ON THE BRIDGE OF THE NOSE TO PROTECT FROM SUNBURN.

USE TO POLISH YOUR TEXAN BAR.

ATTRACT THE ATTENTION OF A VICAR.

BRUSH YOUR TEETH.

SELLOTAPE TO THE WINDOW TO CONFUSE BURGLARS.

A FRIEND TO CROCUSSES.

TIM TRYING TO CATCH A BUTTERFLY

**TIM TRYING TO CATCH SOMEONE
DOING THE BUTTERFLY**

HAMSTER'S FEET

My hamster regularly has a pedicure.
He likes to keep his feet up to scratch.

My local chippy serves hamsters' feet as a delicacy.
It's called Scamper.

Did you know there's a hamster yeti?
He's known to the locals as Littlefoot.

To give my hamster exercise I put glass slippers
on her feet so she can get to the hamster ball.

So this hamster went to the doctor, he said, why
do my hamster skates hurt my feet? He said those aren't
hamster skates. They're vole-erskates.

He said, I've got a corn on my foot what shall I do?
He said store it for the winter.

When a hamster fails to complete a dare he has to wear
tiny gloves on his claws. That's his four feet.

So one hamster says to the other, I like your feet.
Mind if I burrow your shoes?

I invented hamster snow shoes but they didn't make
a big impression.

Dracula eating polystyrene behind a restaurant.

The Archbishop of Canterbury plays with a small yellow trowel and worries about his first flying lesson.

A lumberjack holding some metal railings.

CAR CARE WITH TIM

It's not a coincidence that the word 'care' has the word 'car' in it. Well ... actually it is. We all know how tough it is trying to remove a dent from your car but it's even harder trying to remove a dentist from your car. See below.

You can try talking him out.

Or enticing him out with mouthwash.

If all else fails ... an extraction.

If you ever want to know something about your car you will find most of the answers in your log book.

Finally, always keep hygiene at the top of your car care priorities. Here is a photo of me hoovering my flat.

In Summary: Look after your car because it's a great investment. Although obviously not financially. I once wore some highly inflammable plimsolls. They were my petrol pumps.

HOW THEY MAKE FLAT SCREEN TELLIES

They start by taking an old-fashioned television like the one I'm holding in the picture on the left. Notice the amount of thickness there.

The television is then placed in the immediate path of a steam roller or, as above, a modern roller.

Obviously this type of machinery should be driven by an expert not just any old idiot. The roller is then driven slowly forwards. Almost straight away you will hear a crunching sound. What's on telly? You are.

These three pictures show the sequence of crushing which then occurs.

The driver then dismounts and removes the result from the back of the roller. Another flat-screen telly has been made.

The John Archer
MAGIC PAGE

John Archer is a magician with incredible magical skills. Here he is doing some of his trademark illusions on me. There are no camera tricks on these pages. This all actually happened.

TRICK 1
THE VANISHING PERSON

He's there.

He's gone.

TRICK 2
HAND THROUGH THE BODY

It caused a slightly tickly feeling but other than that I was fine.

This was incredible. Not only did he send me up in the air he also sent part of the lawn up too. Astonishing.

TRICK 4

TRICK 4
THE CARDS ON THE FACE

He sets it up.

He throws the cards.

The cards are on my face.

What an extraordinary afternoon. I've been the victim of magic.

$$2\sin x = \sqrt{3}\,tg\,x$$

DOES IT FLOAT?
NUMBER 453
FIVE PING PONG BALLS SELLOTAPED TO A BRICK

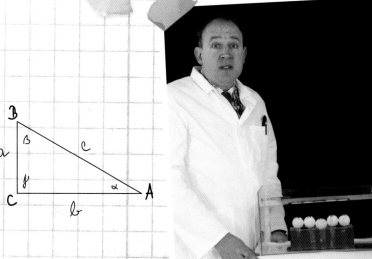

$$= \frac{1}{\sqrt{1 + tg^2\alpha}} = \frac{|cotg\,\alpha|}{\sqrt{1 + cotg^2\alpha}}$$

NO, IT DOESN'T

WHERE DID I PUTT MY PHONE?

We've all been there. And often it's hard to remember the answer isn't it? So what I do is I have a photograph taken every time I putt my phone anywhere. Here are some photos of the places that I'm most likely to putt my phone. Perhaps you recognise them as places you putt your phone too.

Off the top of my wheelie bin

On my stairs

On my sofa

In a large flower pot

Off a garden table

Off the top of the washing machine

Off the lid of a tin of metal polish

ALSO AVAILABLE IN THE SAME SERIES:

Where did I volley my car keys?

Where did I bat my sunglasses?

Where did I ice skate over my wallet?

CHEF VINE

HI THERE,

Chef Vine here. Above is a picture of me holding a hair I found on a piece of beef. Actually it was a living dairy cow. When I removed it she went bonkers. Today's recipe is a very popular one. It's also very simple. There's only two ingredients, but it's crucial how you mix them.

TODAY'S RECIPE: WATER

Ingredients: Hydrogen, Oxygen

Preparation: Measure out the hydrogen so you have twice as much of it as oxygen. Remember not to slice the hydrogen up too finely. If you actually split any of the atoms you will blow up your kitchen and part of the country you are in.

Getting the quantities exactly right is not easy. Some people make that mistake and end up with hydrogen peroxide or hydroxide, neither of which can be used to dilute squash.

Another common mistake is to use twice as much oxygen as hydrogen and that produces o2 which, as you know, is a concert venue.

But if you get it right, you won't regret it. Water tastes so much nicer when it's homemade.

Hokey Cooky!

SING-A-LONG WITH TIM

FAMILY HOLIDAYS

A SONG ABOUT FAMILY HOLIDAYS AND WHAT AN ABSOLUTE SCREAM THEY ARE

A   E7   D   A
Family holidays used to be funny
A   E7   D   A
when I remember them it always makes me laugh.
A   E7   D   D
Ha Ha Ha, Ha Ha Ha, Ha Ha Ha Ha Ha
A   E7   D   A
Ha Ha Ha, Ha Ha Ha, always makes me laugh.

CHORUS

A   D   A
Like the time when we spent a fortnight in France,
A   E7   D   A
my dad bought a beret and he wore it all the time.
A   E7

CHORUS

A   E7   D   A
Like the time when we ordered drinks by the pool
A   E7   D   A
and when they arrived they were completely the wrong
A
ones.

CHORUS

A   E7   D   A
Like the time my uncle fell asleep on the beach
A   E7   D   D
he didn't wake up till the tide was round his waist.
A   E7   D   D
we threw him a rope but it was out of his reach,
A   E7   A
the current swept him out and we never saw him again,

CHORUS

ENDS with a sheepish smile

That's all Forks

IT'S TIME TO SAY GOODBYE,

Yes, that's it. As the Frenchman said when bidding farewell to a man-made lake – Au reservoir.

I hope you've enjoyed your excursion into silliness and your day trip to daft. It's nice to go somewhere different isn't it? I went somewhere different once. I went to a vice factory. It was gripping.

I think you'll agree there's no greater sound in the world than laughter. Unless you've got one of those laughs that sounds like a terrified seagull. That can be quite a scary noise if it happens suddenly just behind you. But the point is as long as you can laugh, all is not lost. I remember once I took my dog for a walk, and while I was out, a storm struck my little cottage and totally flattened it. When I saw the devastation on my return I just had to laugh. Admittedly in that case all WAS lost and my laughter was a tad forced because I was crying a bit as well, but it's still a good point.

Let your hair down once in a while. Put it on the floor and shout, 'Aah! A Hedgehog!' and don't forget to pull a face every now and then. Pull your own face, not someone else's. And for goodness sake talk to trees and flowers. They won't talk back but they can hear you, that's the main thing. Other things that can hear you but won't talk back include ants, the sideboard, flies, and your granny in a huff. There's no harm in being silly. Xanadu, Xanadon't, it's all the same to me.

And finally an apology; I'm sorry this book hasn't answered any of the big questions. Questions like, 'why do people suffer?', 'What is love?' and 'If One Direction split up, which way will they go?' I don't have any of the answers, unless you ask me 'Do you have any of the answers?' In which case my answer's 'no', which I guess means 'yes'. Bye now! (half price later!)

Love Tim

P.S. Leae stay in touch. Oh, sorry, that PS was meant for the word 'please'.

SPECIAL THANKS TO MY GHOST WRITER ANDROOOOOOOOOOOOO

THANKS ALSO TO...

John Archer, JJ, The Colonel, Sheila King, Jobbins, Nick Tinkler, Sonya Vine, Dr G.B.V, Jason Lines, Simon & Judy Parnal, Graham Noon, Rawstone Hire, Alex Crawford, Alison Gerrard, Paul Kerensa, The Flannagans, David Wood, Nuffield Health Centre, Colin Smith, Colin W. Smith, Adina Rotar, Dawn Harris, Aden Pearn, Martin Wainwright, Paul Lassen-Diesen, Karl Hampson, Jane Sturrock for her expert eye (the left one) and all at Orion and thanks to my Mum for knitting sponge finger's red bobble hat.

BACKWORD

Tune signature my that's → ♪ *Vine Tim*

Sillycerely yours,

Attraction the see can't I. Magnets about read rather would people some. Achievable more that make to feathers goose on edition limited a produced have I. You tickles book this hope I readers lovely, so. Prefect nobody's – boy head a have didn't which school old my at say to used they as. 'Smile a crack, on go. Yourself on hard too be don't.' Head own his on cement drying-quick poured had previously hour an half who, cousin my to said I words the of reminded I'm. THIS IS THE ONLY PART WHICH IS THE RIGHT WAY ROUND. Capitals in written is which sentence following the ignore please. Suggestions other for 45 page see. Stranger a to ideally. 'Sprocket giraffe' or 'waffler lozenge' like things say and that about forget to good it's again and now but world serious very a in live we. Also, well as, too stuff other zany daft silly and pictures zany, quizzes daft, jokes silly with it filled I've. It love annual. Annual an like bit a is this. Difference any make won't they because them remove then and. NOW on glasses D3 your put. Silliness of Book Bumper my to Welcome. (THERE YOU IT'S) HERE VINE TIM IT'S.

VIEWERS HELLO!